Horatius Keeps
The Bridge

Thomas Babington,
Lord Macaulay

A Phoenix Paperback

The Lays of Ancient Rome by Thomas Babington, Lord Macaulay,
first published by J. M. Dent in 1954

This edition published in 1996 by Phoenix,
a Division of Orion Books Ltd,
Orion House, 5 Upper St Martin's Lane, London WC2H 9EA

Cover illustration: *Vercingetorix throws down his arms at the feet of
Julius Caesar*, by Lionel Noel Royer, Musée Crozatier, Le Puy en Velay,
France (Bridgeman Art Library, London)

ISBN 1 85799 668 2

Typeset by CentraCet Ltd, Cambridge
Printed in Great Britain by
Clays Ltd, St Ives plc

Contents

Horatius

A lay made about the year of the city CCCLX

1

Lars Porsena of Clusium
  By the Nine Gods he swore
That the great house of Tarquin
  Should suffer wrong no more.
By the Nine Gods he swore it,
  And named a trysting day,
And bade his messengers ride forth,
East and west and south and north,
  To summon his array.

2

East and west and south and north
  The messengers ride fast,
And tower and town and cottage
  Have heard the trumpet's blast.
Shame on the false Etruscan
  Who lingers in his home,
When Porsena of Clusium
  Is on the march for Rome.

3

The horsemen and the footmen
   Are pouring in amain
From many a stately market-place;
   From many a fruitful plain;
From many a lonely hamlet,
   Which, hid by beech and pine,
Like an eagle's nest, hangs on the crest
   Of purple Apennine;

4

From lordly Volaterræ,
   Where scowls the far-famed hold
Piled by the hands of giants
   For godlike kings of old;
From seagirt Populonia,
   Whose sentinels descry
Sardinia's snowy mountain-tops
   Fringing the southern sky;

5

From the proud mart of Pisæ,
   Queen of the western waves,
Where ride Massilia's triremes
   Heavy with fair-haired slaves;
From where sweet Clanis wanders
   Through corn and vines and flowers;

From where Cortona lifts to heaven
    Her diadem of towers.

6

Tall are the oaks whose acorns
    Drop in dark Auser's rill;
Fat are the stags that champ the boughs
    Of the Ciminian hill;
Beyond all streams Clitumnus
    Is to the herdsman dear;
Best of all pools the fowler loves
    The great Volsinian mere.

7

But now no stroke of woodman
    Is heard by Auser's rill;
No hunter tracks the stag's green path
    Up the Ciminian hill;
Unwatched along Clitumnus
    Grazes the milk-white steer;
Unharmed the water fowl may dip
    In the Volsinian mere.

8

The harvests of Arretium,
    This year, old men shall reap;
This year, young boys in Umbro
    Shall plunge the struggling sheep;

And in the vats of Luna,
   This year, the must shall foam
Round the white feet of laughing girls
   Whose sires have marched to Rome.

9

There be thirty chosen prophets,
   The wisest of the land,
Who alway by Lars Porsena
   Both morn and evening stand:
Evening and morn the Thirty
   Have turned the verses o'er,
Traced from the right on linen white
   By mighty seers of yore.

10

And with one voice the Thirty
   Have their glad answer given:
'Go forth, go forth, Lars Porsena;
   Go forth, beloved of Heaven;
Go, and return in glory
   To Clusium's royal dome;
And hang round Nurscia's altars
   The golden shields of Rome.'

11

And now hath every city
   Sent up her tale of men;

The foot are fourscore thousand,
　The horse are thousands ten.
Before the gates of Sutrium
　Is met the great array.
A proud man was Lars Porsena
　Upon the trysting day.

12

For all the Etruscan armies
　Were ranged beneath his eye,
And many a banished Roman,
　And many a stout ally;
And with a mighty following
　To join the muster came
The Tusculan Mamilius,
　Prince of the Latian name.

13

But by the yellow Tiber
　Was tumult and affright:
From all the spacious champaign
　To Rome men took their flight.
A mile around the city,
　The throng stopped up the ways;
A fearful sight it was to see
　Through two long nights and days.

For aged folks on crutches,
   And women great with child,
And mothers sobbing over babes
   That clung to them and smiled,
And sick men borne in litters
   High on the necks of slaves,
And troops of sun-burned husbandmen
   With reaping-hooks and staves,

And droves of mules and asses
   Laden with skins of wine,
And endless flocks of goats and sheep,
   And endless herds of kine,
And endless trains of waggons
   That creaked beneath the weight
Of corn-sacks and of household goods,
   Choked every roaring gate.

Now, from the rock Tarpeian,
   Could the wan burghers spy
The line of blazing villages
   Red in the midnight sky.
The Fathers of the City,
   They sat all night and day,

For every hour some horseman came
    With tidings of dismay.

17

To eastward and to westward
    Have spread the Tuscan bands;
Nor house, nor fence, nor dovecote
    In Crustumerium stands.
Verbenna down to Ostia
    Hath wasted all the plain;
Astur hath stormed Janiculum,
    And the stout guards are slain.

18

I wis, in all the Senate,
    There was no heart so bold,
But sore it ached, and fast it beat,
    When that ill news was told.
Forthwith up rose the Consul,
    Up rose the Fathers all;
In haste they girded up their gowns,
    And hied them to the wall.

19

They held a council standing,
    Before the River-Gate;
Short time was there, ye well may guess,
    For musing or debate.

Out spake the Consul roundly:
  'The bridge must straight go down;
For, since Janiculum is lost,
  Nought else can save the town.'

20

Just then a scout came flying,
  All wild with haste and fear:
'To arms! to arms! Sir Consul:
  Lars Porsena is here.'
On the low hills to westward
  The Consul fixed his eye,
And saw the swarthy storm of dust
  Rise fast along the sky.

21

And nearer fast and nearer
  Doth the red whirlwind come;
And louder still and still more loud,
From underneath that rolling cloud,
Is heard the trumpet's war-note proud,
  The trampling, and the hum.
And plainly and more plainly
  Now through the gloom appears,
Far to left and far to right,
In broken gleams of dark-blue light,
The long array of helmets bright,
  The long array of spears.

And plainly and more plainly,
  Above that glimmering line,
Now might ye see the banners
  Of twelve fair cities shine;
But the banner of proud Clusium
  Was highest of them all,
The terror of the Umbrian,
  The terror of the Gaul.

And plainly and more plainly
  Now might the burghers know,
By port and vest, by horse and crest,
  Each warlike Lucumo.
There Cilnius of Arretium
  On his fleet roan was seen;
And Astur of the four-fold shield,
Girt with the brand none else may wield,
Tolumnius with the belt of gold,
And dark Verbenna from the hold
  By reedy Thrasymene.

Fast by the royal standard,
  O'erlooking all the war,
Lars Porsena of Clusium
  Sat in his ivory car.

By the right wheel rode Mamilius,
    Prince of the Latian name;
And by the left false Sextus,
    That wrought the deed of shame.

25

But when the face of Sextus
    Was seen among the foes,
A yell that rent the firmament
    From all the town arose.
On the house-tops was no woman
    But spat towards him and hissed,
No child but screamed out curses,
    And shook its little fist.

26

But the Consul's brow was sad,
    And the Consul's speech was low,
And darkly looked he at the wall,
    And darkly at the foe.
'Their van will be upon us
    Before the bridge goes down;
And if they once may win the bridge,
    What hope to save the town?'

27

Then out spake brave Horatius,
    The Captain of the Gate:

'To every man upon this earth
  Death cometh soon or late.
And how can man die better
  Than facing fearful odds,
For the ashes of his fathers,
  And the temples of his Gods,

28

'And for the tender mother
  Who dandled him to rest,
And for the wife who nurses
  His baby at her breast,
And for the holy maidens
  Who feed the eternal flame,
To save them from false Sextus
  That wrought the deed of shame?

29

'Hew down the bridge, Sir Consul,
  With all the speed ye may;
I, with two more to help me,
  Will hold the foe in play.
In yon strait path a thousand
  May well be stopped by three.
Now who will stand on either hand,
  And keep the bridge with me?'

30

Then out spake Spurius Lartius;
   A Ramnian proud was he:
'Lo, I will stand at thy right hand,
   And keep the bridge with thee.'
And out spake strong Herminius;
   Of Titian blood was he:
'I will abide on thy left side,
   And keep the bridge with thee.'

31

'Horatius,' quoth the Consul,
   'As thou sayest, so let it be.'
And straight against that great array
   Forth went the dauntless Three.
For Romans in Rome's quarrel
   Spared neither land nor gold,
Nor son nor wife, nor limb nor life,
   In the brave days of old.

32

Then none was for a party;
   Then all were for the state;
Then the great man helped the poor,
   And the poor man loved the great:
Then lands were fairly portioned;
   Then spoils were fairly sold:

The Romans were like brothers
  In the brave days of old.

33

Now Roman is to Roman
  More hateful than a foe,
And the Tribunes beard the high,
  And the Fathers grind the low.
As we wax hot in faction,
  In battle we wax cold:
Wherefore men fight not as they fought
  In the brave days of old.

34

Now while the Three were tightening
  Their harness on their backs,
The Consul was the foremost man
  To take in hand an axe:
And Fathers mixed with Commons
  Seized hatchet, bar, and crow,
And smote upon the planks above,
  And loosed the props below.

35

Meanwhile the Tuscan army,
  Right glorious to behold,
Come flashing back the noonday light,
Rank behind rank, like surges bright

Of a broad sea of gold.
Four hundred trumpets sounded
  A peal of warlike glee,
As that great host, with measured tread,
And spears advanced, and ensigns spread,
Rolled slowly towards the bridge's head,
  Where stood the dauntless Three.

36

The Three stood calm and silent,
  And looked upon the foes,
And a great shout of laughter
  From all the vanguard rose:
And forth three chiefs came spurring
  Before that deep array;
To earth they sprang, their swords they drew,
And lifted high their shields, and flew
  To win the narrow way;

37

Aunus from green Tifernum,
  Lord of the Hill of Vines;
And Seius, whose eight hundred slaves
  Sicken in Ilva's mines;
And Picus, long to Clusium
  Vassal in peace and war,
Who led to fight his Umbrian powers
From that grey crag where, girt with towers,

The fortress of Nequinum lowers
   O'er the pale waves of Nar.

38

Stout Lartius hurled down Aunus
   Into the stream beneath;
Herminius struck at Seius,
   And clove him to the teeth;
At Picus brave Horatius
   Darted one fiery thrust;
And the proud Umbrian's gilded arms
   Clashed in the bloody dust.

39

Then Ocnus of Falerii
   Rushed on the Roman Three;
And Lausulus of Urgo,
   The rover of the sea;
And Aruns of Volsinium,
   Who slew the great wild boar,
The great wild boar that had his den
Amidst the reeds of Cosa's fen,
And wasted fields, and slaughtered men,
   Along Albinia's shore.

40

Herminius smote down Aruns:
   Lartius laid Ocnus low:

Right to the heart of Lausulus
    Horatius sent a blow.
'Lie there,' he cried, 'fell pirate!
    No more, aghast and pale,
From Ostia's walls the crowd shall mark
The track of thy destroying bark.
No more Campania's hinds shall fly
To woods and caverns when they spy
    Thy thrice accursed sail.'

41

But now no sound of laughter
    Was heard among the foes.
A wild and wrathful clamour
    From all the vanguard rose.
Six spears' lengths from the entrance
    Halted that deep array,
And for a space no man came forth
    To win the narrow way.

42

But hark! the cry is Astur:
    And lo! the ranks divide;
And the great Lord of Luna
    Comes with his stately stride.
Upon his ample shoulders
    Clangs loud the four-fold shield,

And in his hand he shakes the brand
   Which none but he can wield.

43

He smiled on those bold Romans
   A smile serene and high;
He eyed the flinching Tuscans,
   And scorn was in his eye.
Quoth he, 'The she-wolf's litter
   Stand savagely at bay:
But will ye dare to follow,
   If Astur clears the way?'

44

Then, whirling up his broadsword
   With both hands to the heights
He rushed against Horatius,
   And smote with all his might,
With shield and blade Horatius
   Right deftly turned the blow.
The blow, though turned, came yet too nigh;
It missed his helm, but gashed his thigh:
The Tuscans raised a joyful cry
   To see the red blood flow.

45

He reeled, and on Herminius
   He leaned one breathing-space;

Then, like a wild cat mad with wounds
    Sprang right at Astur's face.
Through teeth, and skull, and helmet
    So fierce a thrust he sped,
The good sword stood a hand-breadth out
    Behind the Tuscan's head.

46

And the great Lord of Luna
    Fell at that deadly stroke,
As falls on Mount Alvernus
    A thunder smitten oak.
Far o'er the crashing forest
    The giant arms lie spread;
And the pale augurs, muttering low,
    Gaze on the blasted head.

47

On Astur's throat Horatius
    Right firmly pressed his heel,
And thrice and four times tugged amain,
    Ere he wrenched out the steel.
'And see,' he cried, 'the welcome,
    Fair guests, that waits you here!
What noble Lucumo comes next
    To taste our Roman cheer?'

But at his haughty challenge
  A sullen murmur ran,
Mingled of wrath, and shame, and dread,
  Along that glittering van.
There lacked not men of prowess,
  Nor men of lordly race;
For all Etruria's noblest
  Were round the fatal place.

But all Etruria's noblest
  Felt their hearts sink to see
On the earth the bloody corpses,
  In the path the dauntless Three:
And, from the ghastly entrance
  Where those bold Romans stood,
All shrank, like boys who unaware,
Ranging the woods to start a hare,
Come to the mouth of the dark lair
Where, growling low, a fierce old bear
  Lies amidst bones and blood.

Was none who would be foremost
  To lead such dire attack:
But those behind cried 'Forward!'
  And those before cried 'Back!'

And backward now and forward
  Wavers the deep array;
And on the tossing sea of steel,
To and fro the standards reel;
And the victorious trumpet-peal
  Dies fitfully away.

51

Yet one man for one moment
  Strode out before the crowd;
Well known was he to all the Three,
  And they gave him greeting loud.
'Now welcome, welcome, Sextus!
  Now welcome to thy home!
Why dost thou stay, and turn away?
  Here lies the road to Rome.'

52

Thrice looked he at the city;
  Thrice looked he at the dead;
And thrice came on in fury,
  And thrice turned back in dread:
And, white with fear and hatred,
  Scowled at the narrow way
Where, wallowing in a pool of blood,
  The bravest Tuscans lay.

53

But meanwhile axe and lever
    Have manfully been plied;
And now the bridge hangs tottering
    Above the boiling tide.
'Come back, come back, Horatius!'
    Loud cried the Fathers all.
'Back, Lartius! back, Herminius!
    Back, ere the ruin fall!'

54

Back darted Spurius Lartius;
    Herminius darted back:
And, as they passed, beneath their feet
    They felt the timbers crack.
But when they turned their faces,
    And on the farther shore
Saw brave Horatius stand alone,
    They would have crossed once more.

55

But with a crash like thunder
    Fell every loosened beam,
And, like a dam, the mighty wreck
    Lay right athwart the stream:
And a long shout of triumph
    Rose from the walls of Rome,

As to the highest turret-tops
    Was splashed the yellow foam.

56

And, like a horse unbroken
    When first he feels the rein,
The furious river struggled hard,
    And tossed his tawny mane,
And burst the curb and bounded,
    Rejoicing to be free,
And whirling down, in fierce career,
Battlement, and plank, and pier,
    Rushed headlong to the sea.

57

Alone stood brave Horatius,
    But constant still in mind;
Thrice thirty thousand foes before,
    And the broad flood behind.
'Down with him!' cried false Sextus,
    With a smile on his pale face.
'Now yield thee,' cried Lars Porsena,
    'Now yield thee to our grace!'

58

Round turned he, as not deigning
    Those craven ranks to see;
Nought spake he to Lars Porsena,

To Sextus nought spake he;
But he saw on Palatinus
    The white porch of his home;
And he spake to the noble river
    That rolls by the towers of Rome.

59

'Oh, Tiber! father Tiber!
    To whom the Romans pray,
A Roman's life, a Roman's arms,
    Take thou in charge this day!'
So he spake, and speaking sheathed
    The good sword by his side,
And with his harness on his back,
    Plunged headlong in the tide.

60

No sound of joy or sorrow
    Was heard from either bank;
But friends and foes in dumb surprise,
With parted lips and straining eyes,
    Stood gazing where he sank;
And when above the surges
    They saw his crest appear,
All Rome sent forth a rapturous cry,
And even the ranks of Tuscany
    Could scarce forbear to cheer.

But fiercely ran the current,
    Swollen high by months of rain:
And fast his blood was flowing;
    And he was sore in pain,
And heavy with his armour,
    And spent with changing blows:
And oft they thought him sinking,
    But still again he rose.

Never, I ween, did swimmer,
    In such an evil case,
Struggle through such a raging flood
    Safe to the landing place.
But his limbs were borne up bravely
    By the brave heart within,
And our good father Tiber
    Bare bravely up his chin.

'Curse on him!' quoth false Sextus;
    'Will not the villain drown?
But for this stay, ere close of day
    We should have sacked the town!'
'Heaven help him!' quoth Lars Porsena,
    'And bring him safe to shore;

For such a gallant feat of arms
　　Was never seen before.'

64

And now he feels the bottom;
　　Now on dry earth he stands;
Now round him throng the Fathers;
　　To press his gory hands;
And now, with shouts and clapping,
　　And noise of weeping loud,
He enters through the River-Gate,
　　Borne by the joyous crowd.

65

They gave him of the corn-land,
　　That was of public right,
As much as two strong oxen
　　Could plough from morn till night;
And they made a molten image,
　　And set it up on high,
And there it stands unto this day
　　To witness if I lie.

66

It stands in the Comitium,
　　Plain for all folk to see;
Horatius in his harness,
　　Halting upon one knee:

And underneath is written,
    In letters all of gold,
How valiantly he kept the bridge
    In the brave days of old.

67

And still his name sounds stirring
    Unto the men of Rome,
As the trumpet-blast that cries to them
    To charge the Volscian home;
And wives still pray to Juno
    For boys with hearts as bold
As his who kept the bridge so well
    In the brave days of old.

68

And in the nights of winter,
    When the cold north winds blow,
And the long howling of the wolves
    Is heard amidst the snow;
When round the lonely cottage
    Roars loud the tempest's din,
And the good logs of Algidus
    Roar louder yet within;

69

When the oldest cask is opened,
    And the largest lamp is lit;

When the chestnuts glow in the embers,
    And the kid turns on the spit;
When young and old in circle
    Around the firebrands close;
When the girls are weaving baskets,
    And the lads are shaping bows;

70

When the goodman mends his armour,
    And trims his helmet's plume;
When the goodwife's shuttle merrily
    Goes flashing through the loom;
With weeping and with laughter
    Still is the story told,
How well Horatius kept the bridge
    In the brave days of old.

From The Battle of The Lake Regillus

*A lay sung at the feast of Castor and Pollux on the
Ides of Quintilis, in the year of the city* CCCCLI

I

Ho, trumpets, sound a war-note!
    Ho, lictors, clear the way!
The Knights will ride, in all their pride,
    Along the streets today.

Today the doors and windows
    Are hung with garlands all,
From Castor in the Forum,
    To Mars without the wall.
Each Knight is robed in purple,
    With olive each is crowned;
A gallant war-horse under each
    Paws haughtily the ground.
While flows the Yellow River,
    While stands the Sacred Hill,
The proud Ides of Quintilis
    Shall have such honour still.
Gay are the Martian Kalends:
    December's Nones are gay:
But the proud Ides, when the squadron rides,
    Shall be Rome's whitest day.

2

Unto the Great Twin Brethren
    We keep this solemn feast.
Swift, swift, the Great Twin Brethren
    Came spurring from the east.
They came o'er wild Parthenius
    Tossing in waves of pine,
O'er Cirrha's dome, o'er Adria's foam,
    O'er purple Apennine,
From where with flutes and dances
    Their ancient mansion rings,

In lordly Lacedæmon,
    The City of two kings,
To where, by Lake Regillus,
    Under the Porcian height,
All in the lands of Tusculum,
    Was fought the glorious fight.

3

Now on the place of slaughter
    Are cots and sheepfolds seen,
And rows of vines, and fields of wheat,
    And apple-orchards green:
The swine crush the big acorns
    That fall from Corne's oaks.
Upon the turf by the Fair Fount
    The reaper's pottage smokes.
The fisher baits his angle;
    The hunter twangs his bow;
Little they think on those strong limbs
    That moulder deep below.
Little they think how sternly
    That day the trumpets pealed;
How in the slippery swamp of blood
    Warrior and war-horse reeled;
How wolves came with fierce gallop,
    And crows on eager wings,
To tear the flesh of captains,
    And peck the eyes of kings;

How thick the dead lay scattered
    Under the Porcian height;
How through the gates of Tusculum
    Raved the wild stream of flight;
And how the Lake Regillus
    Bubbled with crimson foam,
What time the Thirty Cities
    Came forth to war with Rome.

4

But, Roman, when thou standest
    Upon that holy ground,
Look thou with heed on the dark rock
    That girds the dark lake round.
So shalt thou see a hoof-mark
    Stamped deep into the flint:
It was no hoof of mortal steed
    That made so strange a dint:
There to the Great Twin Brethren
    Vow thou thy vows, and pray
That they, in tempest and in fight,
    Will keep thy head alway.

5

Since last the Great Twin Brethren
    Of mortal eyes were seen,
Have years gone by an hundred
    And fourscore and thirteen.

That summer a Virginius
   Was Consul first in place;
The second was stout Aulus,
   Of the Posthumian race.
The Herald of the Latines
   From Gabii came in state:
The Herald of the Latines
   Passed through Rome's Eastern Gate:
The Herald of the Latines
   Did in our Forum stand;
And there he did his office,
   A sceptre in his hand.

6

'Hear, Senators and people
   Of the good town of Rome:
The Thirty Cities charge you
   To bring the Tarquins home
And if ye still be stubborn,
   To work the Tarquins wrong,
The Thirty Cities warn you,
   Look that your walls be strong.'

7

Then spake the Consul Aulus,
   He spake a bitter jest:
'Once the jays sent a message
   Unto the eagle's nest: –

31

Now yield thou up thine eyrie
  Unto the carrion-kite,
Or come forth valiantly, and face
  The jays in deadly fight. –
Forth looked in wrath the eagle;
  And carrion-kite and jay,
Soon as they saw his beak and claw,
  Fled screaming far away.'

8

The Herald of the Latines
  Hath hied him back in state:
The Fathers of the City
  Are met in high debate.
Then spake the elder Consul,
  An ancient man and wise
'Now hearken, Conscript Fathers,
  To that which I advise.
In seasons of great peril
  'Tis good that one bear sway;
Then choose we a Dictator,
  Whom all men shall obey.
Camerium knows how deeply
  The sword of Aulus bites
And all our city calls him
  The man of seventy fights.
Then let him be Dictator
  For six months and no more,

And have a Master of the Knights
    And axes twenty-four.'

9

So Aulus was Dictator,
    The man of seventy fights;
He made Æbutius Elva
    His Master of the Knights.
On the third morn thereafter,
    At dawning of the day,
Did Aulus and Æbutius
    Set forth with their array,
Sempronius Atratinus
    Was left in charge at home
With boys, and with grey-headed men,
    To keep the walls of Rome.
Hard by the Lake Regillus
    Our camp was pitched at night:
Eastward a mile the Latines lay,
    Under the Porcian height.
Far over hill and valley
    Their mighty host was spread;
And with their thousand watch-fires
    The midnight sky was red.

10

Up rose the golden morning
    Over the Porcian height,

The proud Ides of Quintilis
    Marked evermore with white.
Not without secret trouble
    Our bravest saw the foes;
For girt by threescore thousand spears,
    The thirty standards rose.
From every warlike city
    That boasts the Latian name,
Foredoomed to dogs and vultures,
    That gallant army came;
From Setia's purple vineyards,
    From Norba's ancient wall,
From the white streets of Tusculum,
    The proudest town of all;
From where the Witch's Fortress
    O'erhangs the dark-blue seas;
From the still glassy lake that sleeps
    Beneath Aricia's trees –
Those trees in whose dim shadow
    The ghastly priest doth reign,
The priest who slew the slayer,
    And shall himself be slain;
From the drear banks of Ufens,
    Where flights of marsh-fowl play,
And buffaloes lie wallowing
    Through the hot summer's day;
From the gigantic watch-towers,
    No work of earthly men,

Whence Cora's sentinels o'erlook
   The never-ending fen;
From the Laurentian jungle,
   The wild hog's reedy home;
From the green steeps whence Anio leaps
   In floods of snow-white foam.

11

Aricia, Cora, Norba,
   Velitræ with the might
Of Setia and of Tusculum,
   Were marshalled on the right:
The leader was Mamilius,
   Prince of the Latian name;
Upon his head a helmet
   Of red gold shone like flame:
High on a gallant charger
   Of dark-grey hue he rode;
Over his gilded armour
   A vest of purple flowed,
Woven in the land of sunrise
   By Syria's dark-browed daughters,
And by the sails of Carthage brought
   Far o'er the southern waters.

12

Lavinium and Laurentum
   Had on the left their post,

With all the banners of the marsh,
    And banners of the coast.
Their leader was false Sextus,
    That wrought the deed of shame:
With restless pace and haggard face
    To his last field he came.
Men said he saw strange visions
    Which none beside might see;
And that strange sounds were in his ears
    Which none might hear but he.
A woman fair and stately,
    But pale as are the dead,
Oft through the watches of the night
    Sat spinning by his bed.
And as she plied the distaff,
    In a sweet voice and low,
She sang of great old houses,
    And fights fought long ago.
So spun she, and so sang she,
    Until the east was grey,
Then pointed to her bleeding breast,
    And shrieked, and fled away.

13

But in the centre thickest
    Were ranged the shields of foes,
And from the centre loudest
    The cry of battle rose.

There Tibur marched and Pedum
    Beneath proud Tarquin's rule,
And Ferentinum of the rock,
    And Gabii of the pool.
There rode the Volscian succours:
    There, in a dark stern ring,
The Roman exiles gathered close
    Around the ancient king.
Though white as Mount Soracte,
    When winter nights are long,
His beard flowed down o'er mail and belt,
    His heart and hand were strong:
Under his hoary eyebrows
    Still flashed forth quenchless rage:
And, if the lance shook in his gripe,
    'Twas more with hate than age.
Close at his side was Titus
    On an Apulian steed,
Titus, the youngest Tarquin,
    Too good for such a breed.

14

Now on each side the leaders
    Gave signal for the charge;
And on each side the footmen
    Strode on with lance and targe;
And on each side the horsemen
    Struck their spurs deep in gore

And front to front the armies
    Met with a mighty roar:
And under that great battle
    The earth with blood was red;
And, like the Pomptine fog at morn,
    The dust hung overhead;
And louder still and louder
    Rose from the darkened field
The braying of the war-horns,
    The clang of sword and shield,
The rush of squadrons sweeping
    Like whirlwinds o'er the plain,
The shouting of the slayers,
    And screeching of the slain.

A Radical War Song
(1820)

Awake, arise, the hour is come,
    For rows and revolutions;
There's no receipt like pike and drum
    For crazy constitutions.
Close, close the shop! Break, break the loom,
    Desert your hearths and furrows,
And throng in arms to seal the doom
    Of England's rotten boroughs.

We'll stretch that tort'ring Castlereagh
    On his own Dublin rack, sir;
We'll drown the King in Eau de vie,
    The Laureate in his sack, sir.
Old Eldon and his sordid hag
    In molten gold we'll smother,
And stifle in his own green bag
    The Doctor and his brother.

In chains we'll hang in fair Guildhall
    The City's famed Recorder,
And next on proud St. Stephen's fall,
    Though Wynne should squeak to order.
In vain our tyrants then shall try
    To 'scape our martial law, sir;
In vain the trembling Speaker cry
    That 'Strangers must withdraw,' sir.

Copley to hang offends no text;
    A rat is not a man, sir:
With schedules and with tax bills next
    We'll bury pious Van, sir.
The slaves who loved the Income Tax,
    We'll crush by scores, like mites, sir,
And him, the wretch who freed the blacks,
    And more enslaved the whites, sir.

The peer shall dangle from his gate,
  The bishop from his steeple,
Till all recanting, own, the State
  Means nothing but the People.
We'll fix the church's revenues
  On Apostolic basis,
One coat, one scrip, one pair of shoes
  Shall pay their strange grimaces.

We'll strap the bar's deluding train
  In their own darling halter,
And with his big church bible brain
  The parson at the altar.
Hail glorious hour, when fair Reform
  Shall bless our longing nation,
And Hunt receive commands to form
  A new administration.

Carlisle shall sit enthroned, where sat
  Our Cranmer and our Secker;
And Watson show his snow-white hat
  In England's rich Exchequer.
The breast of Thistlewood shall wear
  Our Wellesley's star and sash, man;
And many a mausoleum fair
  Shall rise to honest Cashman.

Then, then beneath the nine-tailed cat
    Shall they who used it writhe, sir;
And curates lean, and rectors fat,
    Shall dig the ground they tithe, sir.
Down with your Bayleys, and your Bests,
    Your Giffords, and your Gurneys:
We'll clear the island of the pests,
    Which mortals name attorneys.

Down with your sheriffs, and your mayors,
    Your registrars, and proctors,
We'll live without the lawyer's cares,
    And die without the doctor's.
No discontented fair shall pout
    To see her spouse so stupid;
We'll tread the torch of Hymen out,
    And live content with Cupid.

Then, when the high-born and the great
    Are humbled to our level,
On all the wealth of Church and State,
    Like aldermen, we'll revel.
We'll live when hushed the battle's din,
    In smoking and in cards, sir,
In drinking unexcised gin,
    And wooing fair Poissardes, sir.

Sermon in a Churchyard
(1825)

Let pious Damon take his seat,
    With mincing step, and languid smile,
And scatter from his 'kerchief sweet,
    Sabæan odours o'er the aisle;
And spread his little jewelled hand,
    And smile round all the parish beauties,
And pat his curls, and smooth his band,
    Meet prelude to his saintly duties.

Let the thronged audience press and stare,
    Let stifled maidens ply the fan,
Admire his doctrines and his hair,
    And whisper 'What a good young man!'
While he explains what seems most clear,
    So clearly that it seems perplexed,
I'll stay, and read my sermon here;
    And skulls, and bones, shall be the text.

Art thou the jilted dupe of fame?
    Dost thou with jealous anger pine
Whene'er she sounds some other name,
    With fonder emphasis than thine?
To thee I preach; draw near; attend!
    Look on these bones, thou fool, and see

Where all her scorns and favours end,
    What Byron is, and thou must be.

Dost thou revere, or praise, or trust
    Some clod like those that here we spurn;
Some thing that sprang like thee from dust,
    And shall like thee to dust return?
Dost thou rate statesmen, heroes, wits,
    At one sear leaf or wandering feather?
Behold the black, damp, narrow pits,
    Where they and thou must lie together.

Dost thou beneath the smile or frown
    Of some vain woman bend thy knee?
Here take thy stand, and trample down
    Things that were once as fair as she.
Here rave of her ten thousand graces,
    Bosom, and lip, and eye, and chin,
While, as in scorn, the fleshless faces
    Of Hamiltons and Waldegraves grin.

Whate'er thy losses or thy gains,
    Whate'er thy projects or thy fears,
Whate'er the joys, whate'er the pains,
    That prompt thy baby smiles and tears,
Come to my school, and thou shalt learn,
    In one short hour of placid thought,

A stoicism, more deep, more stern,
　　Than ever Zeno's porch hath taught.

The plots and feats of those that press
　　To seize on titles, wealth, or power,
Shall seem to thee a game of chess,
　　Devised to pass a tedious hour.
What matters it to him who fights
　　For shows of unsubstantial good,
Whether his Kings, and Queens, and Knights,
　　Be things of flesh, or things of wood?

We check, and take; exult and fret;
　　Our plans extend, our passions rise,
Till in our ardour we forget
　　How worthless is the victor's prize.
Soon fades the spell, soon comes the night:
　　Say will it not be then the same,
Whether we played the black or white,
　　Whether we lost or won the game?

Dost thou among these hillocks stray,
　　O'er some dear idol's tomb to moan?
Know that thy foot is on the clay
　　Of hearts once wretched as thy own.
How many a father's anxious schemes,
　　How many rapturous thoughts of lovers,

How many a mother's cherished dreams,
  The swelling turf before thee covers!

Here for the living, and the dead,
  The weepers and the friends they weep,
Hath been ordained the same cold bed,
  The same dark night, the same long sleep.
Why shouldest thou writhe, and sob, and rave
  O'er those, with whom thou soon must be?
Death his own sting shall cure – the grave
  Shall vanquish its own victory.

Here learn that all the griefs and joys,
  Which now torment, which now beguile,
Are children's hurts, and children's toys,
  Scarce worthy of one bitter smile.
Here learn that pulpit, throne, and press,
  Sword, sceptre, lyre, alike are frail,
That science is a blind man's guess,
  And History a nurse's tale.

Here learn that glory and disgrace,
  Wisdom and folly, pass away,
That mirth hath its appointed space,
  That sorrow is but for a day;
That all we love, and all we hate,
  That all we hope, and all we fear,

Each mood of mind, each turn of fate,
    Must end in dust and silence here.

The Country Clergyman's Trip to Cambridge

An election ballad
(1827)

As I sate down to breakfast in state,
    At my living of Tithing-cum-Boring,
With Betty beside me to wait,
    Came a rap that almost beat the door in.
I laid down my basin of tea,
    And Betty ceased spreading the toast,
'As sure as a gun, sir,' said she,
'That must be the knock of the post.'

A letter – and free – bring it here –
    I have no correspondent who franks.
No! yes! Can it be? Why, my dear,
    'Tis our glorious, our Protestant Bankes.
'Dear sir, as I know you desire
    That the Church should receive due protection,
I humbly presume to require
    Your aid at the Cambridge election.

'It has lately been brought to my
      knowledge,
   That the Ministers fully design
To suppress each cathedral and college,
   And eject every learned divine.
To assist this; detestable scheme
   Three nuncios from Rome are come over;
They left Calais on Monday by steam,
   And landed to dinner at Dover.

'An army of grim Cordeliers,
   Well furnished with relics and vermin,
Will follow, Lord Westmoreland fears,
   To effect what their chiefs may determine.
Lollard's bower, good authorities say,
   Is again fitting up for a prison;
And a wood-merchant told me today
   'Tis a wonder how faggots have risen.

'The finance scheme of Canning contains
   A new Easter-offering tax;
And he means to devote all the gains
   To a bounty on thumb-screws and racks.
Your living, so neat and compact –
   Pray, don't let the news give you pain! –
Is promised, I know for a fact,
To an olive-faced Padre from Spain.'

I read, and I felt my heart bleed,
  Sore wounded with horror and pity;
So I flew, with all possible speed,
  To our Protestant champion's committee.
True gentlemen, kind and well-bred!
  No fleering! no distance! no scorn!
They asked after my wife who is dead,
  And my children who never were born.

They then, like high-principled Tories,
  Called our Sovereign unjust and unsteady,
And assailed him with scandalous stories,
  Till the coach for the voters was ready.
That coach might be well called a casket
  Of learning and brotherly love:
There were parsons in boot and in basket;
  There were parsons below and above.

There were Sneaker and Griper, a pair
  Who stick to Lord Mulesby like leeches;
A smug chaplain of plausible air,
  Who writes my Lord Goslingham's speeches.
Dr Buzz, who alone is a host,
  Who, with arguments weighty as lead,
Proves six times a week in the Post
  That flesh somehow differs from bread.

Dr Nimrod, whose orthodox toes
    Are seldom withdrawn from the stirrup;
Dr Humdrum, whose eloquence flows,
    Like droppings of sweet poppy syrup;
Dr Rosygill puffing and fanning,
    And wiping away perspiration;
Dr Humbug, who proved Mr. Canning
    The beast in St John's Revelation.

A layman can scarce form a notion
    Of our wonderful talk on the road;
Of the learning, the wit, and devotion,
    Which almost each syllable showed:
Why divided allegiance agrees
    So ill with our free constitution;
How Catholics swear as they please,
    In hope of the priest's absolution;

How the Bishop of Norwich had bartered
    His faith for a legate's commission;
How Lyndhurst, afraid to be martyr'd,
    Had stooped to a base coalition;
How Papists are cased from compassion
    By bigotry, stronger than steel;
How burning would soon come in fashion,
    And how very bad it must feel.

We were all so much touched and excited
    By a subject so direly sublime,
That the rules of politeness were slighted,
    And we all of us talked at a time;
And in tones, which each moment grew
        louder,
    Told how we should dress for the show,
And where we should fasten the powder,
    And if we should bellow or no.

Thus from subject to subject we ran,
    And the journey passed pleasantly o'er,
Till at last Dr Humdrum began;
    From that time I remember no more.
At Ware he commenced his prelection,
    In the dullest of clerical drones;
And when next I regained recollection
    We were rumbling o'er Trumpington stones.

Song
(1827)

O stay, Madonna! stay;
    'Tis not the dawn of day
That marks the skies with yonder opal streak:
    The stars in silence shine;

Then press thy lips to mine,
And rest upon my neck thy fervid cheek.

O sleep, Madonna! sleep;
    Leave me to watch and weep
O'er the sad memory of departed joys,
    O'er hope's extinguished beam,
    O'er fancy's vanished dream,
O'er all that nature gives and man destroys.

O wake, Madonna! wake;
    Even now the purple lake
Is dappled o'er with amber flakes of light;
    A glow is on the hill;
    And every trickling rill
In golden threads leaps down from yonder height.

O fly, Madonna! fly,
    Lest day and envy spy
What only love and night may safely know:
    Fly, and tread softly, dear!
    Lest those who hate us hear
The sounds of thy light footsteps as they go.

The Armada
(1832)

A Fragment

Attend, all ye who list to hear our noble England's
     praise;
I tell of the thrice famous deeds she wrought in ancient
     days,
When that great fleet invincible against her bore in vain
The richest spoils of Mexico, the stoutest hearts of
     Spain.

It was about the lovely close of a warm summer day,
There came a gallant merchant-ship full sail to Plymouth
     Bay;
Her crew hath seen Castile's black fleet, beyond
     Aurigny's isle,
At earliest twilight, on the waves lie heaving many a
     mile.
At sunrise she escaped their van, by God's especial
     grace;
And the tall Pinta, till the noon, had held her close in
     chase.
Forthwith a guard at every gun was placed along the
     wall;
The beacon blazed upon the roof of Edgecumbe's lofty

hall;

Many a light fishing-bark put out to pry along the coast,
And with loose rein and bloody spur rode inland many a
    post.
With his white hair unbonneted, the stout old sheriff
    comes;
Behind him march the halberdiers; before him sound the
    drums;
His yeomen round the market cross make clear an ample
    space;
For there behoves him to set up the standard of Her
    Grace.
And haughtily the trumpets peal, and gaily dance the
    bells,
As slow upon the labouring wind the royal blazon
    swells.
Look how the Lion of the sea lifts up his ancient crown,
And underneath his deadly paw treads the gay lilies
    down.
So stalked he when he turned to flight, on that famed
    Picard field,
Bohemia's plume, and Genoa's bow, and Cæsar's eagle
    shield.
So glared he when at Agincourt in wrath he turned to
    bay,
And crushed and torn beneath his claws the princely
    hunters lay.
Ho! strike the flagstaff deep, sir Knight: ho! scatter
    flowers, fair maids:

Ho! gunners, fire a loud salute: ho! gallants, draw your
   blades:
Thou sun, shine on her joyously; ye breezes, waft her
   wide;
Our glorious SEMPER EADEM, the banner of our pride.

   The freshening breeze of eve unfurled that banner's
      massy fold;
The parting gleam of sunshine kissed that haughty scroll
   of gold;
Night sank upon the dusky beach, and on the purple sea,
Such night in England ne'er had been, nor e'er again
   shall be.
From Eddystone to Berwick bounds, from Lynn to
   Milford Bay,
That time of slumber was as bright and busy as the day;
For swift to east and swift to west the ghastly warflame
   spread,
High on St Michael's Mount it shone: it shone on
   Beachy Head.
Far on the deep the Spaniard saw, along each southern
   shire,
Cape beyond cape, in endless range, those twinkling
   points of fire.
The fisher left his skiff to rock on Tamar's glittering
   waves:
The rugged miners poured to war from Mendip's sunless
   caves:

O'er Longleat's towers, o'er Cranbourne's oaks, the fiery
    herald flew:
He roused the shepherds of Stonehenge, the rangers of
    Beaulieu.
Right sharp and quick the bells all night rang out from
    Bristol town,
And ere the day three hundred horse had met on Clifton
    down;
The sentinel on Whitehall gate looked forth into the
    night,
And saw o'erhanging Richmond Hill the streak of
    blood-red light.
Then bugle's note and cannon's roar the deathlike
    silence broke,
And with one start, and with one cry, the royal city
    woke.
At once on all her stately gates arose the answering
    fires;
At once the wild alarum clashed from all her reeling
    spires;
From all the batteries of the Tower. pealed loud the
    voice of fear;
And all the thousand masts of Thames sent back a
    louder cheer:
And from the furthest wards was heard the rush of
    hurrying feet,
And the broad streams of pikes and flags rushed down
    each roaring street;

And broader still became the blaze, and louder still the
    din,
As fast from every village round the horse came spurring
    in:
And eastward straight from wild Blackheath the warlike
    errand went,
And roused in many an ancient hall the gallant squires
    of Kent.
Southward from Surrey's pleasant hills flew those bright
    couriers forth;
High on bleak Hampstead's swarthy moor they started
    for the north;
And on, and on, without a pause untired they bounded
    still:
All night from tower to tower they sprang; they sprang
    from hill to hill:
Till the proud peak unfurled the flag o'er Darwin's rocky
    dales,
Till like volcanoes flared to heaven the stormy hills of
    Wales,
Till twelve fair counties saw the blaze on Malvern's
    lonely height,
Till streamed in crimson on the wind the Wrekin's crest
    of light,
Till broad and fierce the star came forth on Ely's stately
    fane,
And tower and hamlet rose in arms o'er all the
    boundless plain;

Till Belvoir's lordly terraces the sign to Lincoln sent,
And Lincoln sped the message on o'er the wide vale of
    Trent;
Till Skiddaw saw the fire that burnt on Gaunt's
    embattled pile,
And the red glare on Skiddaw roused the burghers of
    Carlisle.

Epitaph on a Jacobite

(1845)

To my true king I offered free from stain
Courage and faith; vain faith, and courage vain.
For him, I threw lands, honours, wealth, away,
And one dear hope, that was more prized than they.
For him I languished in a foreign clime,
Grey-haired with sorrow in my manhood's prime;
Heard on Lavernia Scargill s whispering trees,
And pined by Arno for my lovelier Tees;
Beheld each night my home in fevered sleep,
Each morning started from the dream to weep;
Till God, who saw me tried too sorely, gave
The resting place I asked, an early grave.
Oh thou, whom chance leads to this nameless stone,
From that proud country which was once mine own,

By those white cliffs I never more must see,
By that dear language which I spake like thee,
Forget all feuds, and shed one English tear
O'er English dust. A broken heart lies here.

A Note on Thomas Babington, Lord Macaulay

Thomas Babington, Lord Macaulay, (1800–59), the poet, British historian and statesman, was born at Rothley Temple, Leicestershire, the son of Zachary Macaulay, the philanthropist. He was educated privately and at Trinity College, Cambridge. In 1825 he began to contribute to the *Edinburgh Review*, when his essay on Milton appeared. He entered Parliament in 1830 and two years later was appointed a commissioner, and a year later secretary of the Board of Control. In 1834, tempted by the large salary that would enable him to save enough to support himself for the rest of his life, he accepted an appointment as a member of the Supreme Council of India, and he stayed there for five years. During this time he assisted in preparing a criminal code for India, which did not, however, become law until the year after his death. On his return to Britain he was returned to Parliament as member for Edinburgh and in 1839 became secretary of war, which office he held for two years. He lost his seat in 1847, but regained it in 1852.

Macaulay published 'Horatius' and 'The Battle of the

Lake Regillus' as part of the *Lays of Ancient Rome* in 1842 and in the following years revised some of his *Edinburgh Review* articles for publication in book form. Since 1839 he had been at work on his *History of England*, which was to deal with the period from the revolution to the death of George III; but it was not until 1848 that the first two volumes appeared, the third and fourth being published seven years later and the fifth posthumously (1861). The *History* was received with a chorus of praise. Its sale was enormous and its vivid style made it eminently readable and induced the reader to overlook the Whig bias that everywhere dominated it. His work is now read rather for its literary style than for its historical value; his search for effect and his prejudices militate against accuracy. As a narrative writer he is of the first rank, as in his description of England in 1685. Macaulay was raised to the peerage in 1857. His tomb is in Westminster Abbey.